RUBANK EDUCATIONAL LIBRARY No. 184

RUBANK
Advanced Method

Eb OR BBb BASS

VOL. II

WM. GOWER
AND
H. VOXMAN

**AN OUTLINED COURSE OF STUDY
DESIGNED TO FOLLOW UP ANY
OF THE VARIOUS ELEMENTARY
AND INTERMEDIATE METHODS**

HAL•LEONARD® CORPORATION
7777 W. BLUEMOUND RD. P.O. BOX 13819 MILWAUKEE, WI 53213

NOTE

THE RUBANK ADVANCED METHOD for E♭ or BB♭ Bass is published in two volumes, the course of study being divided in the following manner:

Vol. I { Keys of B♭, E♭, F, A♭, and C Major.
        { Keys of G, C, D, F, and A Minor.

Vol. II { Keys of D♭, G, G♭, D, C♭, and A Major.
        { Keys of B♭, E, E♭, and B Minor.

PREFACE

THIS METHOD is designed to follow any of the various Elementary and Intermediate instruction series, or Elementary instruction series comprising two or more volumes, depending upon the previous development of the student. The authors have found it necessary in their teaching experience to draw from many sources in order to provide a progressive course of study. The present publication assembles in two volumes, the material essential to a well-rounded musical development.

THE OUTLINES, one of which is included in each of the respective volumes, tend to afford an objective picture of the student's progress. They will facilitate the ranking of members in a large ensemble or they may serve as a basis for awards of merit. In addition, a one-sided development along strictly technical or strictly melodic lines is avoided. The use of these outlines, however, is not imperative and they may be discarded at the discretion of the teacher.

Wm. Gower — H. Voxman

PRACTICE AND GRADE REPORT

SECOND SEMESTER

Student's Name _____   Date _____

Week	Sun.	Mon.	Tue.	Wed.	Thu.	Fri.	Sat.	Total	Parent's Signature	Grade
1										
2										
3										
4										
5										
6										
7										
8										
9										
10										
11										
12										
13										
14										
15										
16										
17										
18										
19										
20										

Semester Grade _____

Instructor's Signature _____

FIRST SEMESTER

Student's Name _____   Date _____

Week	Sun.	Mon.	Tue.	Wed.	Thu.	Fri.	Sat.	Total	Parent's Signature	Grade
1										
2										
3										
4										
5										
6										
7										
8										
9										
10										
11										
12										
13										
14										
15										
16										
17										
18										
19										
20										

Semester Grade _____

Instructor's Signature _____

Chromatic Fingering Chart for BBb Bass

① The B♮ or C♭ below the staff is too sharp. Flatten this tone enough to make it in good tune.

② The C on the second space is usually too flat. Correct this in slow passages by using 1st and 3rd valves.

③ The D on the third line will sometimes be too flat. Use 1st and 2nd valves to improve this in slow passages.

TABLE OF HARMONICS

Chromatic Fingering Chart for E♭ Bass

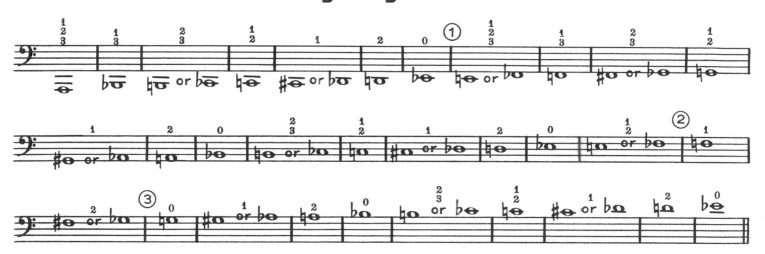

① The E♮ or F♭ below the staff is too sharp. Flatten this tone enough to make it in good tune.

② The F on the fourth line is usually too flat. Correct this in slow passages by using 1st and 3rd valves.

③ The G on the fourth space will sometimes be too flat. Use 1st and 2nd valves to improve this in slow passages.

TABLE OF HARMONICS

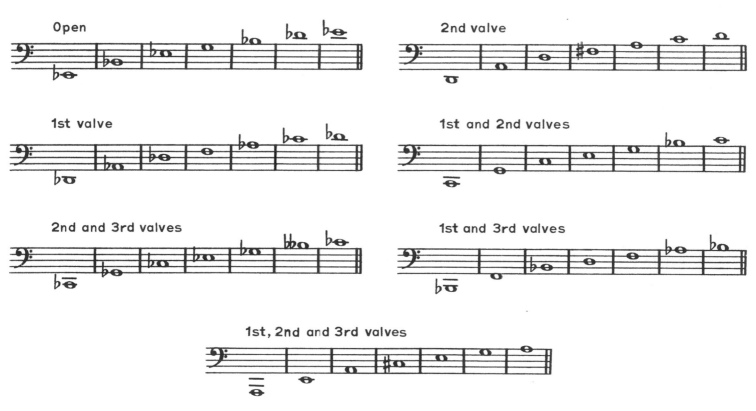

Fingerings for the tones above high E♭:

1566-87-PL

OUTLINE
OF
RUBANK ADVANCED METHOD
FOR
BBb BASS, Vol. II
BY
Wm. Gower and H. Voxman

UNIT	SCALES and ARPEGGIOS	(Key)	MELODIC INTERPRE- TATION	ARTICU- LATION	FLEXIBILITY and TONGUING		ORNAMENTS	SOLOS	UNIT COM- PLETED
1	8 (1) 10 (9)	Db	30 (1)	47 (1)	60 (1)	70 (1)	75 (1)	82 (1)	
2	8 (3) 11 (10)	Db	30 (1)	47 (2)	60 (1)	70 (1)	75 (1)	82 (1)	
3	9 (4) (6) 11 (11)	Db	31 (3)	48 (3)	60 (1)	70 (2)	75 (2)	82 (1)	
4	10 (7) 11 (12)	Db	32 (5)	48 (4)	60 (2)	70 (3)	75 (2)	82 (1)	
5	11 (13) (14) 12 (18)	bb	33 (7)	48 (5)	60 (2)	70 (4)	75 (3)	82 (1)	
6	12 (15) (19)	bb	34 (9)	49 (7)	60 (2)	70 (4)	75 (3)	82 (1)	
7	12 (16) 13 (20)	bb	34 (9)	49 (7)	60 (3)	70 (5)	76 (4)	82 (2)	
8	13 (21) 15 (29)	G	35 (10)	49 (8)	60 (3)	70 (5)	76 (4)	82 (2)	
9	13 (23) 15 (30)	G	36 (12)	50 (9)	61 (4)	71 (6)	76 (5)	82 (2)	
10	14 (25) 15 (31)	G	36 (13)	50 (10)	61 (4)	71 (6)	76 (5)	82 (2)	
11	14 (27) 15 (32)	G	36 (13)	50 (10)	61 (5)	71 (7)	77 (6)	82 (2)	
12	15 (33) 17 (37)	e	37 (15)	51 (12)	61 (5)	71 (7)	77 (6)	82 (2)	
13	16 (34) 17 (38)	e	37 (15)	51 (12)	61 (6)	71 (8)	77 (7)	84 (3)	
14	16 (35) 17 (39) (40)	e	38 (16)	52 (13)	61 (7)	71 (8)	77 (8)	84 (3)	
15	18 (42)	Gb	38 (17)	52 (15)	61 (8)	72 (9)	77 (8)	84 (3)	
16	18 (43) 20 (48)	Gb	38 (18)	53 (16)	61 (9)	72 (9)	78 (9) (10)	84 (3)	
17	18 (44) 20 (49)	Gb	39 (19)	53 (17)	61 (10)	72 (9)	78 (11)	84 (3)	
18	19 (46) 20 (50)	Gb	39 (19)	53 (17)	61 (11)	72 (10)	78 (11)	84 (3)	
19	20 (51) 21 (54)	eb	39 (20)	54 (18)	61 (12)	72 (10)	79 (12) (13)	85 (4)	
20	20 (52) 21 (55)	eb	40 (21)	54 (19)	62 (13)	72 (11)	79 (14)	85 (4)	
21	20 (53) 21 (56)	eb	40 (21)	54 (20)	62 (13)	72 (11)	79 (14)	85 (4)	
22	21 (57) 23 (62)	D	41 (22)	55 (21)	62 (13)	73 (12)	79 (15)	85 (4)	
23	21 (58) 23 (63)	D	41 (23)	55 (22)	62 (13)	73 (12)	79 (15)	85 (4)	
24	22 (59) 23 (64)	D	42 (24)	56 (23)	62 (13)	73 (13)	79 (16)	85 (4)	
25	23 (61) (65)	D	42 (24)	56 (23)	63 (14)	73 (14)	80 (17)	88 (6)	
26	24 (66) 25 (70)	b	43 (26)	56 (24)	63 (14)	73 (14)	80 (18)	88 (6)	
27	24 (67) 25 (71)	b	44 (28)	56 (24)	63 (14)	73 (15)	80 (19)	88 (6)	
28	24 (68) 25 (72)	b	44 (28)	57 (25)	63 (14)	73 (15)	80 (19)	88 (6)	
29	25 (73) 27 (79)	Cb	44 (29)	57 (26)	63 (14)	74 (16)	81 (20)	88 (6)	
30	25 (74) 27 (80)	Cb	44 (29)	57 (27)	63 (14)	74 (16)	81 (21)	88 (6)	
31	26 (76) 27 (81)	Cb	45 (30)	58 (28)	64 (15)	74 (17)	81 (22)	92 (8)	
32	26 (77) 27 (82)	Cb	45 (30)	58 (28)	64 (15)	74 (17)	81 (23)	92 (8)	
33	27 (83)	A	46 (32)	58 (29)	64 (15)	74 (18)	81 (24)	92 (8)	
34	28 (84) 29 (89)	A	46 (32)	59 (30)	64 (15)	74 (18)	81 (25)	92 (8)	
35	28 (86) 29 (90)	A	46 (33)	59 (31)	64 (15)	74 (19)	81 (26)	92 (8)	
36	29 (87) (91)	A	46 (33)	59 (31)	64 (15)	74 (19)	81 (27)	92 (8)	

NUMERALS designate page number.

ENCIRCLED NUMERALS designate exercise number.

COMPLETED EXERCISES may be indicated by crossing out the rings, thus, ⊗.

1566 - 87

OUTLINE
OF
RUBANK ADVANCED METHOD
FOR
Eb BASS, Vol. II
BY
Wm. Gower and H. Voxman

UNIT	SCALES and ARPEGGIOS	(Key)	MELODIC INTERPRE-TATION	ARTICU-LATION	FLEXIBILITY and TONGUING		ORNAMENTS	SOLOS	UNIT COMPLETED
1	8 (2) 10 (9)	Db	30 (2)	47 (1)	65 (1)	70 (1)	75 (1)	82 (1)	
2	9 (4) 11 (10)	Db	31 (4)	47 (2)	65 (1)	70 (1)	75 (1)	82 (1)	
3	9 (5) (6) 11 (11)	Db	32 (6)	48 (3)	65 (1)	70 (2)	75 (2)	82 (1)	
4	10 (8) 11 (12)	Db	32 (6)	48 (4)	65 (2)	70 (3)	75 (2)	82 (1)	
5	11 (13) (14)	bb	34 (8)	48 (5)	65 (2)	70 (4)	75 (3)	82 (1)	
6	12 (15) (18) (19)	bb	34 (9)	49 (6)	65 (2)	70 (4)	75 (3)	82 (1)	
7	12 (17) 13 (20)	bb	34 (9)	49 (7)	66 (3)	70 (5)	76 (4)	82 (2)	
8	13 (22) 15 (29)	G	35 (10)	49 (8)	66 (3)	70 (5)	76 (4)	82 (2)	
9	13 (24) 15 (30)	G	35 (11)	50 (9)	66 (4)	71 (6)	76 (5)	82 (2)	
10	14 (26) 15 (31)	G	37 (14)	50 (11)	66 (4)	71 (6)	76 (5)	82 (2)	
11	15 (28) (32)	G	37 (14)	50 (11)	66 (5)	71 (7)	77 (6)	82 (2)	
12	15 (33) 17 (37)	e	37 (15)	51 (12)	66 (5)	71 (7)	77 (6)	82 (2)	
13	16 (34) 17 (38)	e	37 (15)	51 (12)	66 (6)	71 (8)	77 (7)	84 (3)	
14	16 (36) 17 (39) (40)	e	38 (16)	52 (13)	66 (7)	71 (8)	77 (8)	84 (3)	
15	17 (41)	Gb	38 (17)	52 (14)	66 (8)	72 (9)	77 (8)	84 (3)	
16	18 (43) 20 (48)	Gb	38 (18)	53 (16)	66 (9)	72 (9)	78 (9) (10)	84 (3)	
17	19 (45) 20 (49)	Gb	39 (19)	53 (17)	66 (10)	72 (9)	78 (11)	84 (3)	
18	19 (47) 20 (50)	Gb	39 (19)	53 (17)	67 (11)	72 (10)	78 (11)	84 (3)	
19	20 (51) 21 (54)	eb	39 (20)	54 (18)	67 (12)	72 (10)	79 (12) (13)	86 (5)	
20	20 (52) 21 (55)	eb	40 (21)	54 (19)	67 (13)	72 (11)	79 (14)	86 (5)	
21	20 (53) 21 (56)	eb	40 (21)	54 (20)	67 (13)	72 (11)	79 (14)	86 (5)	
22	21 (57) 23 (62)	D	41 (22)	55 (21)	67 (13)	73 (12)	79 (15)	86 (5)	
23	21 (58) 23 (63)	D	41 (23)	55 (22)	67 (13)	73 (12)	79 (15)	86 (5)	
24	22 (60) 23 (64)	D	42 (24)	56 (23)	67 (13)	73 (13)	79 (16)	86 (5)	
25	23 (61) (65)	D	42 (24)	56 (23)	68 (14)	73 (14)	80 (17)	90 (7)	
26	24 (66) 25 (70)	b	42 (25)	56 (24)	68 (14)	73 (14)	80 (18)	90 (7)	
27	24 (67) 25 (71)	b	43 (27)	56 (24)	68 (14)	73 (15)	80 (19)	90 (7)	
28	24 (69) 25 (72)	b	43 (27)	57 (25)	68 (14)	73 (15)	80 (19)	90 (7)	
29	25 (73) 27 (79)	Cb	44 (29)	57 (26)	68 (14)	74 (16)	81 (20)	90 (7)	
30	25 (75) 27 (80)	Cb	44 (29)	57 (27)	68 (14)	74 (16)	81 (21)	90 (7)	
31	26 (76) 27 (81)	Cb	45 (30)	58 (28)	68 (15)	74 (17)	81 (22)	92 (8)	
32	26 (78) 27 (82)	Cb	45 (30)	58 (28)	68 (15)	74 (17)	81 (23)	92 (8)	
33	27 (83)	A	45 (31)	58 (29)	68 (15)	74 (18)	81 (24)	92 (8)	
34	28 (85) 29 (89)	A	45 (31)	59 (30)	68 (15)	74 (18)	81 (25)	92 (8)	
35	29 (87) (90)	A	46 (33)	59 (31)	68 (15)	74 (19)	81 (26)	92 (8)	
36	29 (88) (91)	A	46 (33)	59 (31)	68 (15)	74 (19)	81 (27)	92 (8)	

NUMERALS designate page number.

ENCIRCLED NUMERALS designate exercise number.

COMPLETED EXERCISES may be indicated by crossing out the rings, thus, ⊗.

1566-87

Scales and Arpeggios

Db Major

10

Various articulations may be used in the chromatic, the interval, and the chord studies, at the instructor's option.

12

Diminished 7th Chord

20

G Major

BBb Bass only

21

simile

simile

Eb Bass only

22

simile

simile

BBb Bass only

23

simile

Eb Bass only

24

simile

1566 - 87

14

18

22

B Minor

Scale in Thirds

70

Common Chord

71

Diminished 7th Chord

72

Cb Major

73

simile

simile

74 BBb Bass only

simile

simile

75 Eb Bass only

simile

simile

28

1566 - 87

Studies in Melodic Interpretation

The following studies are designed to aid in the development of the student's interpretative ability. Careful attention to the marks of expression is essential to effective use of the material. Pencil the technically difficult passages and devote extra time to their mastery.

In rhythmic music in the more rapid tempi (marches, dances, etc.), tones that are equal divisions of the beat are played somewhat detached (staccato). Tones that equal a beat or are multiples of a beat are held full value. Tones followed by rests are usually held full value. This point should be especially observed in slow music.

1566-87-PL

BORGHI

34

Allegretto

HÖHNE

March time

KLING

BOLERO

ROSSINI

MULLER

KLING

KREUTZER

SIDOW

DUREAU

Lively

HÖHNE

Majestically

PFLEGER

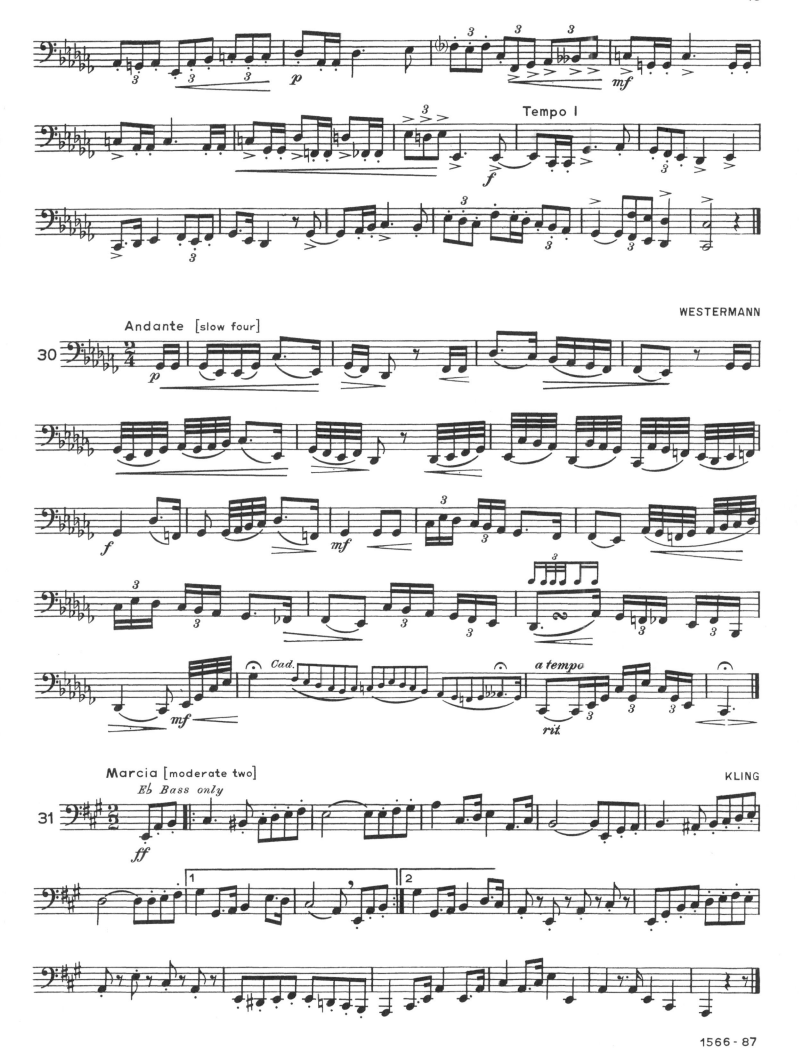

46

GALLAY

DUREAU

1566 - 87

Studies in Articulation

The material for this section has been taken from standard methods for bass and for other brass instruments.

In all exercises where no tempo is indicated, the student should play the study as rapidly as is consistent with tonal control and technical accuracy.

Fingerings above notes for E♭ Bass, below notes for BB♭ Bass.

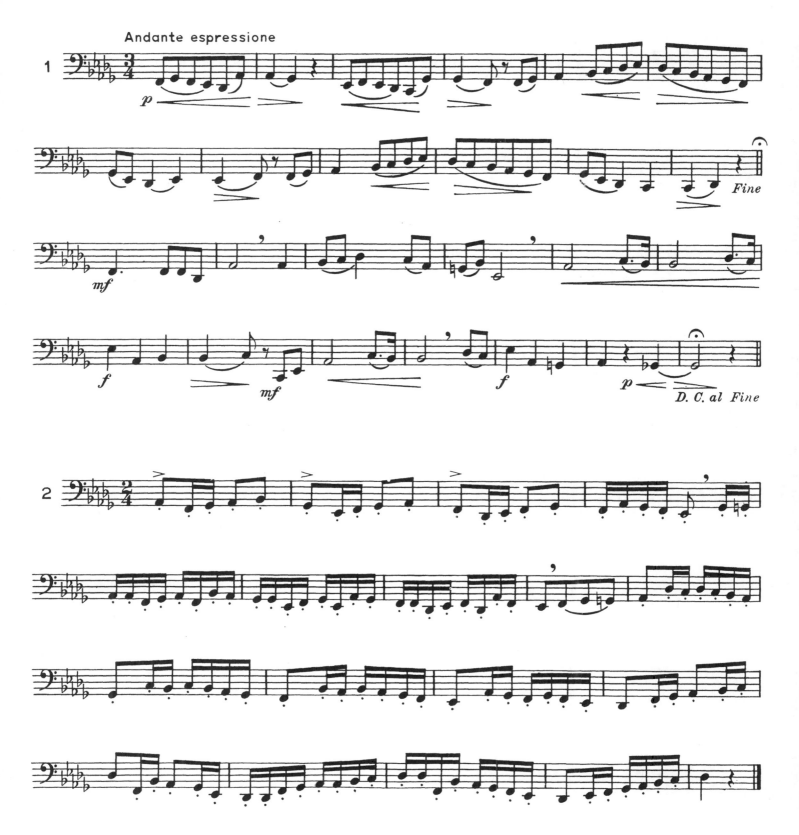

48

52

56

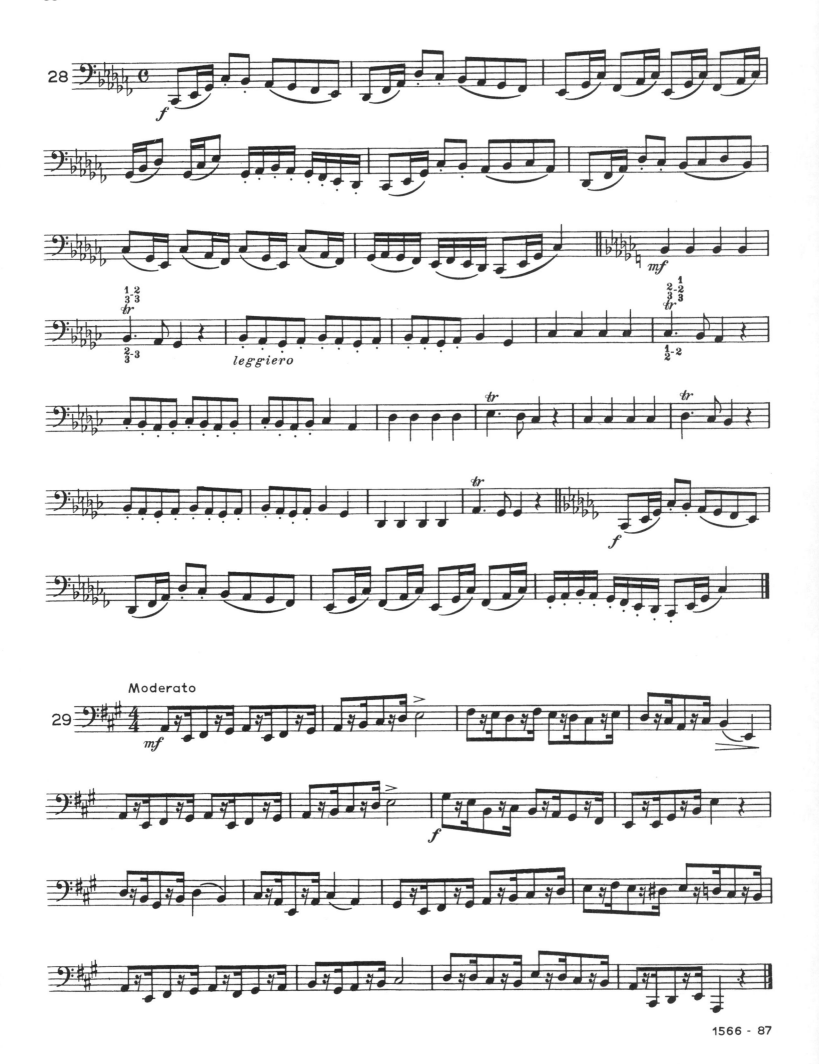

Flexibility Exercises for BB♭ Bass

Flexibility Exercises for BB♭ Bass (Cont'd)

Flexibility Exercises for BBb Bass (Cont'd)

Flexibility Exercises for E♭ Bass

Flexibility Exercises for E♭ Bass (Cont'd)

Tonguing Exercises
TRIPLE TONGUING and DOUBLE TONGUING

Triple tonguing is used when triplets are to be played at a speed that is too fast for single tonguing. The pattern of syllables used for this kind of tonguing is: Tu Tu Ku, Tu Tu Ku, etc.

Double tonguing is used when duplets are to be played at a speed that is too fast for single tonguing. The pattern of syllables in this case is: Tu Ku, Tu Ku, etc.

To develop a technic for either Triple or Double Tonguing it is recommended that the Ku attacks be practiced separately from the Tu attacks until a good tone can be produced on both syllables.   The student may then proceed to combine the Tu and Ku, being particularly careful that both syllables sound with equal clarity. It is advisable to practice slowly at first in order to produce an evenly articulated rhythm. Increase to a faster tempo only as perfection is reached.

PREPARATORY STUDIES

TRIPLE TONGUING

DOUBLE TONGUING

Tu Ku Tu Ku Tu   Tu Ku Tu Ku Tu

74

Musical Ornamentation (Embellishments)

Fingerings above notes for E♭ Bass, below notes for BB♭ Bass.

ARBAN

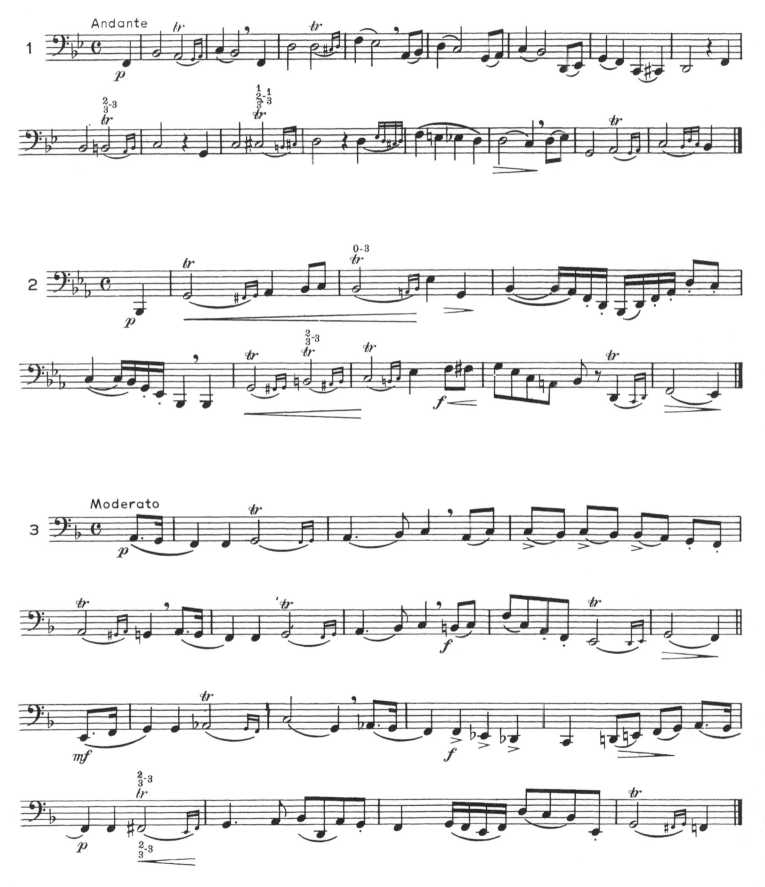

ARBAN

Long Grace Notes (Appoggiatura)

The Turn (Gruppetto)

GALLAY

In the music of Wagner it is sometimes necessary to play turns that begin on the lower instead of the upper note. The symbol for this inverted turn is ⟳. The turn in the excerpt from "Rienzi" was not written thus originally by Wagner but is usually interpreted in the manner indicated.

In the music of the time of Bach and Handel (1685-1759), cadences frequently contain the rhythmic figure or . The time value of the dot is not trilled, the execution being etc. It should be added that trills of this period should generally begin with the upper note of the trill.

SARABAND

SOLOS
Premier Solo de Concours

Eb or BBb Bass

R. MANIET

Air Gai

E♭ or BBb Bass

G. P. BERLIOZ

Andante et Allegro

Eb or BBb Bass

ROBERT CLÉRISSE

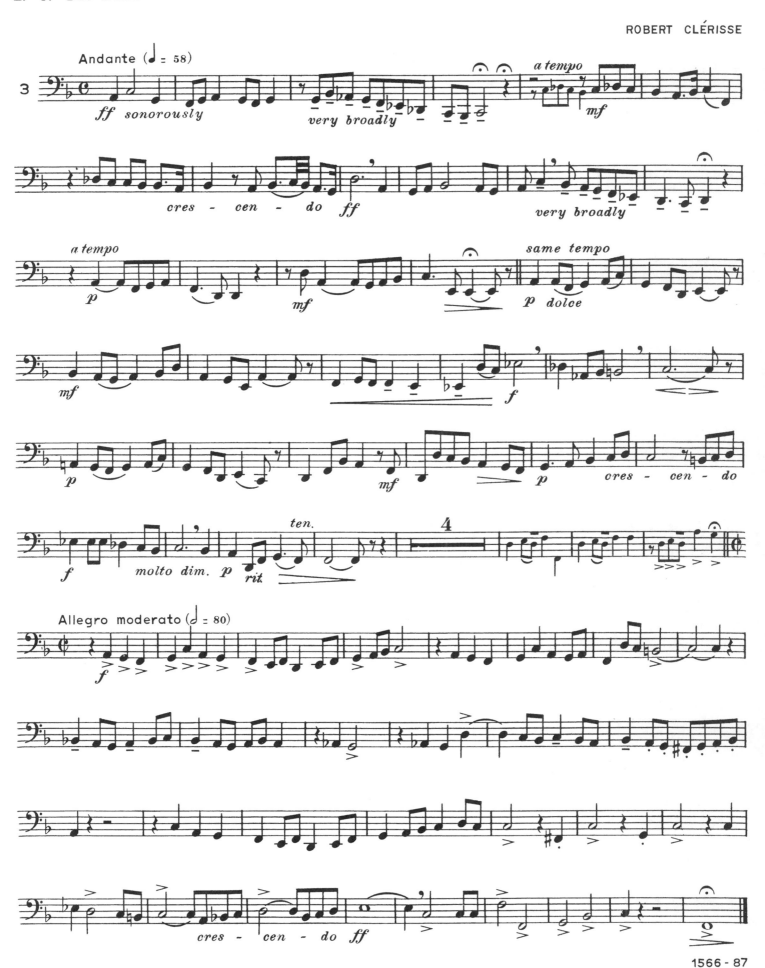

Élégie

BBb Bass

ALEXANDRE J. DUQUESNE

Cavatine

Eb Bass

DEMERSSEMAN, Op. 47

Très largement et avec énergie
[very broadly and with energy]

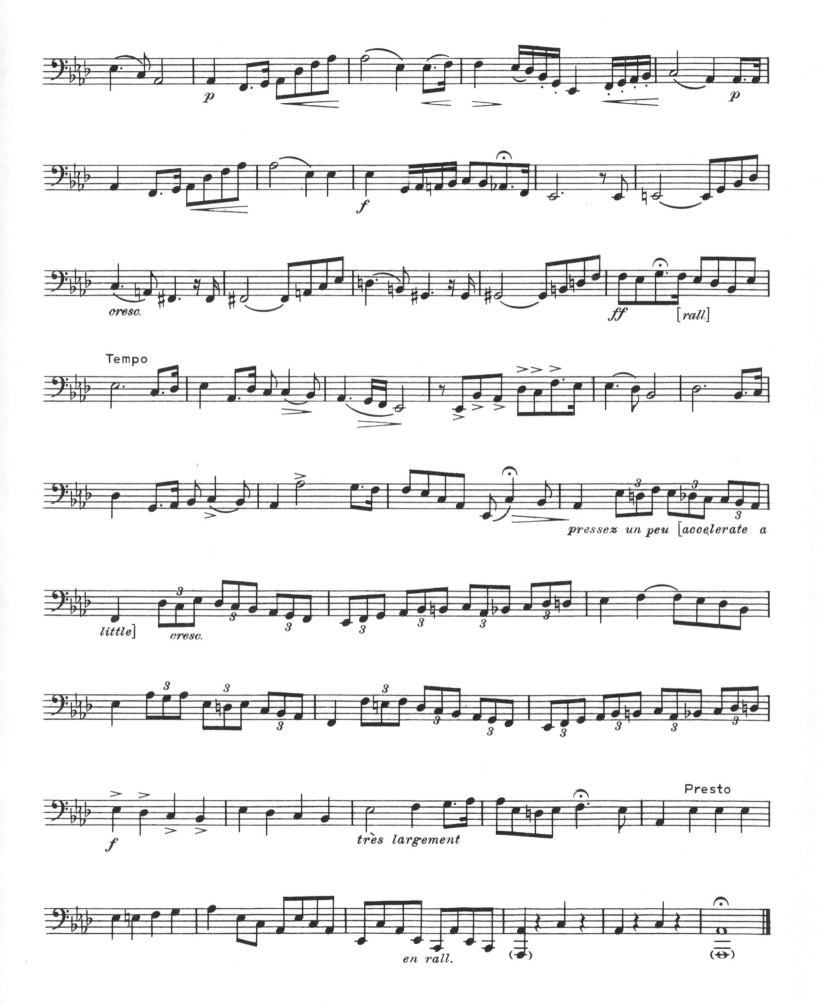

Adagio and Finale
from Concertino

BB♭ Bass

CHARLES GAUCET

FINALE

Morceau de Concours

Eb Bass

G. ALARY, Op. 57

Concertpiece

E♭ or BB♭ Bass

H. PAINPARÉ
Revised by H. Voxman

Tempo di Bolero

Note . . .

Upon completion of this course of study, BBb Bass players who desire to develop further the upper register of their instrument, may review much of the material in this method that is designated for "Eb Bass only," with good result (except the "Flexibility Exercises for Eb Bass").